DIRTY WEEKEND

A Comedy in One Act by Jack Booth

CHARACTERS *(in ord*

Sally
Neal
Mrs Tom
Daphr
Timothy
Tom
Claire

The action takes place in the lounge of Number 13 Melrose Place.

Time: The present. A Friday evening in summer.

PRODUCTION NOTE: The three virtues... Pace, Attack and Clarity.

The lounge of No. 13 Melrose Place. A door upstage in R wall opens onstage from the entrance-hall with staircase. Downstage of the door is an easy-chair. In the centre of the rear wall are french/patio windows with floor-length curtains.

A door downstage in L wall opens offstage into a passageway leading to the kitchen and back door.

Upstage of the door is a sideboard with telephone. Centre stage is a settee facing downstage towards a non-practical television set DC on a low stand. Any other furniture, etc., is optional for set-dressing purposes.

AT RISE: The stage is empty. Both doors are closed as are the windows whose curtains are drawn open.

Outside the windows is BRIGHT EVENING SUNSHINE.

After a few seconds the door R opens and SALLY ENTERS. SALLY is aged 16, a pretty girl with a pert, likeable personality. (Note: It is important that she retains audience sympathy. On the surface she acts/speaks with a certain brash apparent self-confidence and maturity, but basically is equally inexperienced as is Neal although in his case it is only too obvious)She is dressed in a trendily teenage manner but not overtly sexy. She has a sling-bag over one shoulder.

SALLY: *(Moving in URC)* And here we are - home sweet home! What do you think? *(Receiving no reply she turns and calls to R)* Neal! *(Moving back to open doorway to call to Offstage as she faces downstage)* Neal!! *(Putting hands on hips)* Are you coming in or aren't you? If you stand out there much longer looking like the little boy that Santa Claus forgot, you'll have Tommy next door phoning the police. *(Miming speaking into telephone as she moves to UC)* I want to report ever such a queer-looking young chap lurking outside Number 13 Melrose Place. What's he doing? Well he's lurking, isn't he. There's nobody home for the weekend. I think he might be a burglar. *(Calling to R)* Have you closed the front door? *(DOOR SLAMS LOUDLY offstage R. Dropping her shoulder-bag onto settee as she moves above and then L of it)* He has now!

NEAL ENTERS R into open doorway. NEAL is aged 17. His glasses help to give him an owlishly serious appearance and he obviously is ill at ease. He is conventionally dressed in a suit and anorak but with the addition of a woollen football supporter's hat and scarf. In one hand he is carrying a small travel-bag and in the other a wooden rattle adorned with ribbons matching the colours of hat and scarf.

That's it - let everybody know we're here! We could have made a public announcement!

NEAL: *(Subdued)* I'm sorry, Sally. My hand slipped off the knob. I don't look like a burglar.

SALLY: That's true.

NEAL: *(Protesting)* And I'm not queer.

SALLY: I should hope not... otherwise this weekend's going to be a bit of a dead loss.

NEAL: *(Closing the door with some difficulty)* I meant queer-looking. *(She gives a dubious look. He moving to R of settee)* And I wasn't lurking - I was wiping my feet on the outside doormat. *(Dropping travel-bag to floor)* Who's this

Tommy?

SALLY: *(Removing her jacket)* Her next door... *(nodding L)* Mrs Tomkins. We call her Peeping Tommy. *(Dropping jacket onto settee)* Not to her face of course. *(Moving DLC)* Mum says she's a one-woman Neighbourhood Watch. And when Dad was living here he used to say, "What that Tommy doesn't know about what goes on in Melrose Place not only isn't worth knowing - it almost certainly hasn't happened".

NEAL: *(Nervously)* Do you think she saw us come in?

SALLY: I hope not! I couldn't see her peeping through her front window curtains where she spends most of her time. Perhaps she's on a tea-break. Well, make yourself at home. We're here until Sunday afternoon, you know.

NEAL: *(Anything but 'at home')* Are you sure it's alright, Sally.... us being here... like this... just the two of us?

SALLY: How many do you want - a mass orgy? Of course it's alright. I live here, don't I?

NEAL: *(Unconvinced)* What if your mother comes home?

SALLY: She won't - I've already told you. *(Giggling as she sits L settee)* But if she did, wouldn't she have a cat-fit! *(He reacts with alarm)* For heaven's sake, relax! Mum won't come back until Sunday evening. She's spending the weekend with somebody she calls Tim.

NEAL: Who's he?

SALLY: Her fancy-man. I think his name's Wainwright.

NEAL: The schoolteacher?

SALLY: Do you know him?

NEAL: I used to be in his class for mathematics.

SALLY: *(Interested)* What's he like? *(Wistfully)* I suppose he's awfully good-looking?

NEAL: *(Flatly)* He's a right wimp.

SALLY: *(Pleased)* Really?

NEAL: That's what we used to call him - "The Wimp"... or Wimpy Wainwright.

SALLY: *(Optimistically)* Shouldn't think he'll last very long. My Dad's real macho.

NEAL: You're hoping that he'll get together again with your mum, aren't you?

SALLY: Of course.

NEAL: Hasn't he got a fancy-woman?

SALLY: *(Strongly)* He wouldn't look at another woman! *(Less positively)* Well, he might look. Aren't you going to take your things off?

NEAL: *(Apprehensively)* Already! I thought we'd talk first. You know - get better acquainted.

SALLY: I didn't mean get undressed, silly! Take your coat off - and that hat and scarf. What's the rattle for?

NEAL: *(Removing hat, coat and scarf)* It's part of my cover-story. *(Proudly)* I thought it made a nice touch.

SALLY: *(Offhandedly)* That depends on the cover-story.

NEAL: I told Mother and Father I was going to watch United at Wembley tomorrow afternoon. It's a charity match or something. *(Spinning the rattle)*

SALLY: *(Alarmed)* Quiet! You'll have Tommy coming round. I didn't think you were interested in football?

NEAL: I'm not - twenty-two men kicking a ball about. But I had to invent something, didn't I? I borrowed these things from Albert Sudbury in exchange for one of my mega-drive games.

SALLY: Star Wars?

NEAL: Teenage Mutant Turtles.

SALLY: *(Aside)* I might have guessed! *(As he stands still awkwardly holding hat, coat, scarf and rattle)* Drop your things on that chair. *(Pointing DR)* Then we'll take them upstairs.

NEAL: *(Quickly checking move DR)* Upstairs?

SALLY: If we hang them in the hall, I wouldn't put it past Peeping Tommy peeping through the letterbox if she gets suspicious.

NEAL: *(Placing hat, coat and scarf on easy-chair DR but still holding rattle)* Why should she?

SALLY: If she hears noises. The house is supposed to be empty, isn't it?

NEAL: What sort of noises?

SALLY: *(Offhandedly)* I don't know. Sit down, Neal, you're making me as nervous as you are.

NEAL: *(Picking up hat, coat and scarf in order to sit in easy chair DR)* I'm not nervous! *(Sitting holding them on his lap)*

SALLY: *(With feeling)* I meant over here... beside me. *(Patting seat of settee)*

NEAL: I'm quite comfy here, thanks all the same. *(His appearance belying his words as he puts rattle on top of the other items he is nursing)* Where does your mother think you are?

SALLY: *(Rising impatiently to DLC)* With Dad... in that grotty little flat. When you think he could still be living here. I'm there most weekends.

NEAL: Why not this weekend?

SALLY: *(Tersely)* Because I'm here with you, aren't I? *(Aside)* And beginning to wonder why!

NEAL: What I meant was... where does your father think you are? As you're here and not there.

SALLY: *(Moving UC)* With Mavis Oldthorpe. Her parents are on holiday. Her dad's in Corfu with some of his mates he goes drinking with. Her mother's at Great Yarmouth.

NEAL: Who with?

SALLY: I didn't ask. Some man, I suppose. Mavis says it's taking their holidays separately that keeps them together.

NEAL: I can't see my parents ever doing that. So your mother thinks you're with your dad... and he thinks....

SALLY: That I'm with Mavis. Simple, isn't it? And you're supposed to be on your way to London if you didn't miss the bus.

NEAL: I said train. I didn't want Mother to worry - I get sick on a bus.

SALLY: What about tomorrow night?

NEAL: I thought about that. I said I'd stay in London at the YMCA and go to a theatre - ballet perhaps or the opera.

SALLY: *(Mischievously)* Or one of those striptease shows in Soho?

NEAL: *(Standing quickly and spilling his clothes)* No, I should never do that!

SALLY: *(Laughing as she moves back downstage L of settee)* I was only teasing. *(Sitting again L end of settee as he picks up rattle and starts to pick up clothes from floor)* Leave them and come and sit next to me. *(Putting her jacket and bag onto floor L of settee as he reluctantly starts to move towards her, carrying rattle)* You won't need that!

NEAL: *(Putting rattle on easy-chair DR)* Isn't it hot in here? *(Starting to move UC)* Perhaps I should open the windows?

SALLY: And perhaps you shouldn't! If Mrs Tomkins is snooping and sees them open, she'll be ringing the police saying we've got burglars. The next thing you know your Mum and Dad will be having to bail you out. Then what about your cover-story? Now will you please sit down!

There is a brief pause as NEAL moves slowly downstage L of settee.

NEAL: *(Avoiding sitting on settee)* What happened?

SALLY: So far - nothing!

NEAL: I meant between your parents. Why they're not living together.

SALLY: *(Rising and moving DRC)* Apparently, they decided to live apart.

NEAL: *(As if making a profound statement)* They must have been incompatible.

SALLY: *(Not really listening)* No, they didn't get on.

NEAL: *(On verge of correcting her, then deciding not to)* What does he do - your Dad?

SALLY: *(Defensively)* He doesn't. He was made redundant twice - both here and at work. *(Firmly)* Now that's quite enough talk, my lad. Time for action! You know what they say - actions speak louder than words. *(Mock-imperiously)* Come here! *(He glances anxiously towards door L as possible means of retreat)* Neal! *(As he turns and sheepishly falls to his knees)* What are you doing?

NEAL: *(Nervously)* You told me to kneel.

SALLY: No I didn't. I said "Neal". That is your name, isn't it? What on earth did you think I wanted you to kneel for?

NEAL: *(Shamefaced as he gets to his feet)* I had no idea.

SALLY: Neither have I... the mind boggles! *(Regarding him keenly)* Are you sure you've done this sort of thing before?

NEAL: *(With feigned bravado)* Many a time!

SALLY: *(Aside)* He could have fooled me!

NEAL: *(Pertinently)* Have you?

As SALLY hesitates, voice of MRS TOMKINS is heard (offstage R)

MRS TOMKINS: *(Offstage)* Hello! Hello, is there somebody in there?

SALLY: *(Whispering cautiously)* It's her! I bet she's shouting through the letterbox. I hope she gets her nose trapped! *(Putting a warning finger to her lips she moves to quietly open door R and then drops onto her knees to peer round the door-jamb towards downstage)*

NEAL: *(Whispering)* Is she there?

SALLY: *(Getting to her feet and moving above settee)* She seems to have gone. Get your things, we're going upstairs.

NEAL: Why?

SALLY: Because a pound to a penny, the next thing she'll be round peeping in these windows.

NEAL: We could close the curtains.

SALLY: *(Sarcastically)* We could switch the telly on at full blast! Hurry up before you have any more bright ideas! *(Picking up her jacket and bag from floor L of settee)*

NEAL crosses downstage to pick up his hat, coat, scarf and rattle DR.

(SALLY moves above settee to R as he touches rattle) And mind that rattle doesn't rattle! *(It does so faintly and he clutches it desperately as he moves towards her at door)* Your bag!

NEAL moves back to pick up his travel-bag and then, crossing below her, Exits R towards upstage.

SALLY quickly looks around room and, having glanced anxiously towards the windows UC, Exits R closing door behind her.

Immediately afterwards MRS TOMKINS ENTERS UC (from offstage L) outside the windows. MRS TOMKINS is a middle-aged, inquisitive-looking woman wearing a long pinafore over her dress and thick, wrinkled stockings.

Her hair is in curlers and partly covered by a headscarf wrapped turban-wise around her head. Moving as closely as possible to the windows and shading her eyes with one hand, she strains her neck to peer shortsightedly around the room. With an exaggerated shrug of frustrated disappointment, she reluctantly Exits to Offstage L.

After a few seconds the door R opens and DAPHNE ENTERS. DAPHNE is in her late 30's and is not in a good mood. She is wearing a well-fitted summer dress and is carrying a lightweight coat and a small week-end case, both of which she dumps unceremoniously onto settee when she moves in above it.

DAPHNE: *(Whispering to Offstage DR as she enters)* Don't slam the door, Timothy.

TIMOTHY ENTERS R. TIMOTHY is in his mid-40's, a rather serious, self-centred individual, apt to speak somewhat pedantically. He is wearing a neat, two-piece suit with shirt and discreet tie. A flight-bag is slung over one shoulder.

TIMOTHY: *(Whispering curtly)* I wasn't going to. *(Closing door)* Why are we whispering?... You said that nobody is here.

DAPHNE: For the same reason that I said don't slam the door. I don't want Mrs Tomkins to know we're here... or it will be all round Melrose Place before bedtime.

TIMOTHY: Who's she, Daphne?

DAPHNE: *(Moving L of settee)* From next door - Mrs Tomkins, superspy! *(As he unslings his flight-bag and sits heavily in easy-chair DR, placing the bag carefully on floor; tersely)* Make yourself at home!

TIMOTHY: Thanks, I'm quite exhausted.

DAPHNE: *(Aside)* That sounds encouraging!

TIMOTHY: I don't see why I had to park the car about half a mile away.

DAPHNE: *(Moving DLC)* The exercise will do you good... anyway it was no more than a hundred yards. If she *(nodding L)* had heard a car pull up outside it would have been "Action Stations" with binoculars at the ready. As it is, I was surprised not to see her front-window curtains move.

TIMOTHY: A curtain-twitcher, is she?

DAPHNE: She knows I'm supposed to be away for the weekend - and Sally of course.

TIMOTHY: How?

DAPHNE: *(Sarcastically)* How! It's like living next door to Mata Hari. You can't keep anything secret.

TIMOTHY: Is there a Mr Mata Hari?

DAPHNE: Apparently there was - until he disappeared. Can you blame him?

TIMOTHY: *(Looking around)* Not a bad little place you've got here.

DAPHNE: *(Sitting on settee)* I'm glad you approve. *(Tautly)* Thought I'd seen the back of it for forty-eight hours.

TIMOTHY: *(Rising and strolling complacently towards the windows UC)* Sorry about that... couldn't be helped.

DAPHNE: Don't go too close to the windows - she might be watching. *(Complaining)* At least you could have phoned and saved me a journey.

TIMOTHY: *(Moving DLC)* I did telephone. I got no answer. You must have already left.

DAPHNE: *(Peevishly)* You should have phoned earlier.

TIMOTHY: How was I to know that Stanley was going to turn up unexpectedly?

DAPHNE: You're his brother - he should have let you know.

TIMOTHY: *(Testily, as he crosses below settee to DRC)* It is his flat and he doesn't happen to be psychic. How was he supposed to know he was going to fall off a ladder?

DAPHNE: *(Unsympathetically)* He should have been more careful.

TIMOTHY: That job was supposed to keep him away for another couple of weeks at least.

DAPHNE: *(Rising and moving DLC)* I don't know why you haven't got a place of your own... like my dear husband did when he departed.

TIMOTHY: You make him sound as though he were dead. Anyway he needed somewhere for his daughter to spend weekends with him. I don't have that problem.

DAPHNE: Sally is not a problem!

TIMOTHY: I didn't say she was, but she would be, wouldn't she, if she was here? Could be embarrassing.

DAPHNE: For you?

TIMOTHY: Me? *(Dissembling)* No, of course not. Why should it? I was thinking of you - and her. It might put ideas into her head.

DAPHNE: She's only sixteen. She hasn't even got a boyfriend yet.

TIMOTHY: *(Moving URC)* I've had girls in my class mothers before then.

DAPHNE: *(Amused)* You dirty old man! Do the school governors know?

TIMOTHY: *(Pompously)* That wasn't funny, Daphne... and not at all in good taste! *(With change of tone)* Anyway, you'll be pleased to hear that I have started to look around for somewhere of my own to live.

DAPHNE: *(Tormenting him)* Finally given up hope that Margaret will take you back?

TIMOTHY: *(To DRC)* I should never go back... not if she begged me on bended knee - the one that's *not* arthritic.

DAPHNE: Tell me, Tim, did you leave voluntarily, or did Margaret throw you out?

TIMOTHY: *(Indignantly)* Certainly not! The decision was taken by mutual agreement.

DAPHNE: I see - she decided and you agreed.

TIMOTHY: If I didn't know you better, Daphne, I should say you were trying to start an argument.

DAPHNE: *(Tersely)* And if you did know me better, you'd be quite sure I was. *(Relenting slightly)* I'm sorry, but I do hate having my plans upset.

TIMOTHY: So that's what this is all about? Was it my fault Stanley fell off the ladder? *(Moving below settee)* He might have broken his neck! You wouldn't have wanted that to happen.

DAPHNE: *(Crossing below him and flinging herself into easy-chair DR)* At least he wouldn't be littering up the flat. He's only broken his arm.

TIMOTHY: He's in a lot of pain. I was far from happy leaving him alone in his hour of need.

DAPHNE: *(Jumping up impetuously and moving URC)* Then why don't you go back and hold his hand? On the arm that isn't broken. *(Moving above settee to ULC)*

TIMOTHY: *(Turning to follow her move)* Come off it, Daphne! You know I'd rather be here with you.

DAPHNE: *(With a sudden change of mood as she moves DLC)* Would you really? I don't know why you put up with me.

TIMOTHY: Nor do I.

DAPHNE: *(Indignant)* What!?

TIMOTHY: It was a joke.

DAPHNE: I really am being an absolute bitch, aren't I?

TIMOTHY: *(In mild reproof)* Not absolutely.

DAPHNE: I'd been so looking forward to spending the weekend with you, after missing out last week.

TIMOTHY: *(Breaking DRC)* It was Mother's birthday and I never miss visiting her.

DAPHNE: You could have taken me with you.

TIMOTHY: *(Hesitantly)* Ah, now that would have been rather tricky. Mother is very old-fashioned... explaining who you are... what you were...

DAPHNE: *(Baldly)* I'm your lover. *(With urgency as she moves below settee)* I want you, Timothy! I need you, Timothy! Now... this very minute! Let's go upstairs!

TIMOTHY: I say, hang on, old girl. Upstairs - here?

DAPHNE: It isn't a bungalow.

TIMOTHY: *(Awkwardly)* It's just that... wouldn't you rather stay down here? The settee looks quite comfortable.

DAPHNE: *(With utmost certitude)* I insist on making love in a bed!

TIMOTHY: *(Unhappily)* But yours... and his?

DAPHNE: He's made his bed... he no longer lies in this one.

TIMOTHY: But all the same... well, it doesn't seem quite right.

DAPHNE: *(Impatiently)* Oh, for heaven's sake, Tim, it's not as if he's suddenly going to walk in here! Now get your things and come along! *(Taking her jacket and case off settee)*

TIMOTHY: *(Picking up his flight-bag)* Shall I take your case?

DAPHNE: *(Crossing below him towards door R)* You'd better save your strength... but you could open the door.

TIMOTHY: Yes, of course. *(Moving to open door and DAPHNE Exits R to Upstage; thoughtfully to himself)* Did I pack my ginseng? *(Exits R, closing door behind him)*

After a few seconds MRS TOMKINS ENTERS UC (From Offstage L) outside windows. She now has a pair of binoculars hanging by a strap on her chest. Raising them to her eyes she scans into the room. Apparently encountering some difficulty, she breathes on the lenses and wipes them on a handkerchief from her apron pocket and again looks into the room before stepping backwards (upstage) to stretch her neck upwards as if looking at a bedroom window. Continuing to look upwards, she moves out of sight to R.

As she does so the door R opens and SALLY ENTERS. Leaving the door open she crosses above settee to open door L and Exits, leaving that door open also.

MRS TOMKINS returns into sight from R, still looking upwards through binoculars. Without stopping to look into the room she Exits UC to Offstage L.

NEAL ENTERS R, closes the door and is moving in to URC as SALLY ENTERS L, now carrying a glass of water. Startled she barely manages to stifle a scream and almost drops the glass.

SALLY: *(Recovering)* Neal! You gave me such a fright! I thought you were still upstairs. *(Closing the door and moving above settee)* Here's your glass of water - I was going to bring it up.

NEAL: *(Feigning)* I - er... I thought I'd save you the trouble.

SALLY: *(As she briskly crosses below him to R he puts out a hand to take the glass but watches it sail past him)* It's no trouble. Come along... back up the apples and pears.

NEAL: I might as well drink it down here.

SALLY: *(Not pleased)* Oh, alright, here you are. *(Holding out glass)*

NEAL: *(Taking it)* Thanks. *(Moving DRC he is on verge of sitting on settee but quickly changes his mind and sits in easy-chair DR)*

SALLY: *(Following him DRC)* Do you have to sit down to drink it?

NEAL: If I swallow too fast I get hiccups. I have to sip very slowly. *(Demonstrating)*

SALLY: *(Moving below settee with an eloquent expression on her face)* As slowly as that? This could take the whole weekend! *(As he continues to sip painfully slowly)* Couldn't you sip just a bit quicker?

NEAL: *(Refusing to do so and looking towards the television set DC)* I wonder what's on the telly?

SALLY: *(Impatiently)* We're not going to find out! *(Turning to study him carefully)* Are you sure you've done this before?

NEAL: *(Obtusely)* Drinking water? Oh, yes, several times every day. Mother says it flushes out the kidneys.

SALLY: *(Incredulously)* Really! *(As he continues to sip slowly; Sally losing control)* Neal! Do please hurry up! *(Breaking DLC)*

Reluctantly NEAL gulps the remaining water and rises. As he moves DC holding out the empty glass he suddenly hiccups.

NEAL: There, you see! What did I tell you? *(Hiccups again)* Now I shall have to have another glass to get rid of these hiccups. *(Again hiccups)*

SALLY: *(Aside)* Not forgetting flushing the kidneys! *(To him)* The kitchen's at the far end of the passage. *(Indicating door DL)*

NEAL crosses below her with the empty glass, opens door and Exits L, leaving door open. He hiccups (Offstage L)

(With resignation) Suppose I'd better go with him or he'll sit in there sipping water till kingdom come. We've already got a hosepipe ban. *(Exits L, closing door)*

After a few seconds the door R opens and TIMOTHY ENTERS, now without his jacket and tie, followed by DAPHNE who is finishing putting on a negligee.

TIMOTHY: *(Apologetically)* It's no use, Daphne, I can't concentrate until I've given Stanley a ring to see if he's alright. You don't mind, do you? *(Looking around the room)*

DAPHNE: *(Displeased)* By all means - if it will help you concentrate. It's over there. *(Indicating sideboard L)* Just as we were getting undressed!

TIMOTHY: *(Moving above settee to pick up telephone)* I couldn't possibly speak to him with no clothes on. *(Making a call)*

DAPHNE: *(Moving DRC)* Why not? For all you know he may have no clothes on.

TIMOTHY: *(Surprised, speaking into telephone)* Who's that? Who? What number have I got? It can't be! It is. Is Stanley there? He's where? In bed. Put him on please. I don't care how inconvenient it is. This is his brother. *(To Daphne, shocked)* He's got a woman there!

DAPHNE: So he probably has got no clothes on. Some women have all the luck.

TIMOTHY: *(About to reproach her but then again speaking into telephone)* It's Timothy of course - how many brothers have you got? Who's that woman? I know her name's Linda, she told me that. She's your girl-friend? I didn't know you had one - not here, I mean. I daresay you have a girl on every job you go to. No, I didn't say were you on the job. Oh, you are! Or rather you were before you were interrupted, I'm sorry. How's your arm? I see, she's a nurse. So you're in good hands. Or rather you were. I did say I was sorry! *(Slamming the phone down and moving DLC)* Would you believe that? The ingratitude! Here I was worrying about him and there he is...

DAPHNE: Undergoing psychotherapy! *(Moving towards open door R)* Now can we please concentrate? Or would you like to ring your mother and ask permission?

TIMOTHY: *(Pedantically)* There is absolutely no need to adopt that tone of voice. Sarcasm is the lowest form of wit.

DAPHNE: *(Pointedly)* Now where have I heard that before! Will you please come along.

TIMOTHY: What's all the rush? We've got the whole weekend.

DAPHNE: At this rate it'll take the whole weekend to even get you started.

TIMOTHY: I do wish you'd be more understanding. I need the right ambience. I can't just perform at the drop of a hat - like a trained seal.

DAPHNE: I should have got a tin of sardines. Well, I'm not wearing a hat and I've dropped everything else. *(Briefly opening the bottom of her negligee)*

TIMOTHY: *(Heavily as he moves below settee towards her)* That's what attracted me to you in the first instance... the refined manner in which you express yourself. *(Crossing below her to Exit R)*

DAPHNE: And there I was thinking it was my animal magnetism! *(Exits R, closing door behind her)*

After a few seconds the door L opens and SALLY ENTERS.

SALLY: *(As she enters)* Now, are you quite sure you've drunk enough? *(Turning to find herself alone)* Neal! *(To herself)* I've lost him again! I shall have to get a collar and chain. *(Moving back to call through open doorway to Offstage L)* Neal! What are you doing?

NEAL: *(Offstage L)* I'm coming.

SALLY: *(To L of settee)* So is Christmas!

NEAL: *(ENTERS L, carrying a glass of water)* I thought I'd better bring another... just in case.

SALLY: What... the tap runs dry?

NEAL: I start hiccuping again.

SALLY: You've only just stopped... and you've had three glasses already. *(Moving R above settee)* Now can we please go back? Talk about flushing your kidneys, you'll be flushing our toilet all night long.

Outside the windows EVENING SUNLIGHT FADES

(Turning to find him lingering by the open doorway L) Now what is it? Don't say you've left the tap dripping.

NEAL: I thought I heard someone in the kitchen... at the back door.

SALLY: It'll be Tommy on her rounds. Hurry up before she's at the windows. *(Opening door R)* Close that door! *(He starts to do so and then suddenly "freezes")* Neal!

NEAL: *(Miserably)* I think I'm going to hiccup again.

SALLY: *(Threateningly)* Don't you dare!

NEAL: I'd better have a sip. *(He slowly does so)*

SALLY: *(Impatiently)* This is where I came in! *(He closes door)* Aren't you going to top it up? *(He starts to open door)* Neal!!!

NEAL: *(As if shot he closes door and moves above settee to L of her; politely, glass in hand)* After you.

SALLY: Not likely, my lad. I want to keep my eyes on you - both of them!

NEAL crosses below her and Exits R, followed by SALLY who closes door behind her.

The door L opens and CLAIRE ENTERS followed by TOM. CLAIRE is in her mid-30's, a fussy, timid woman. She is plainly dressed and is wearing a hat and outdoor coat. She is carrying a small suitcase and a full plastic carrier-bag. TOM is aged about 40, athletic looking and casually dressed in jeans, trainers and a t-shirt under a zip-up jacket. A rucksack is thrown over one shoulder.

CLAIRE: *(Nervously as she moves in to below settee)* Why did we have to sneak in the back door, Tom?

TOM: *(Closing door L)* We didn't sneak in, Claire. We walked in normally.

CLAIRE: I didn't feel normal. I felt as if I was sneaking in... as if we had no right to be here. And I'm not sure we have.

TOM: *(Unconcerned as he moves in)* Whose name is on the mortgage papers?

CLAIRE: *(Putting down case and carrier-bag)* Yours and my sister's, I suppose.

TOM: That's right, mine and Daphne's. So I've every right to be here legally.

CLAIRE: This feels illegal to me.

TOM: The reason we sneaked in at the back door as you put it, apart from me still having the key, was because the front is almost certainly under observation.

CLAIRE: *(Highly nervous)* By the police?

TOM: *(Scornfully)* No, not the police... the local agent for MI5!

CLAIRE: *(Giggling)* Oh, Tom, you are awful! You're pulling my leg. You mean Mrs Tomkins. I'd forgotten about her.

TOM: *(With feeling)* I wish I could! *(Moving above settee to R)* We may as well go straight up.

CLAIRE: *(Uneasily)* Isn't it a bit early. I don't feel at all sleepy.

TOM: *(About to open door R)* Who said anything about sleep?

CLAIRE: Couldn't we sit and talk... to break the ice?

TOM: Ice? I'll soon warm you up.

CLAIRE: *(Hesitantly)* It's not as if we've done it before... not together, I mean.

TOM: Oh, all right - just for five minutes mind. *(Unslinging rucksack as he moves DRC)*

CLAIRE: *(With a nervous little laugh)* To see you anyone would think you were off hiking.

TOM: I haven't heard it called that before. *(Putting rucksack down by easy-chair DR)* Not that there's anybody here to see, is there? *(As she stands hovering awkwardly)* Aren't you going to take your hat and coat off?

CLAIRE: You mustn't rush me, Tom.

TOM: Who's rushing you?

CLAIRE: *(Slowly removing hat and coat)* I can't stand being rushed. That was the cause of the trouble between me and Godfrey. He would insist on rushing me... right from the honeymoon.

TOM: He was impatient.

CLAIRE: We got to the airport at least an hour before we needed to.

TOM: Like I said - he was impatient.

> TOM starts to move as if to sit R end of settee but CLAIRE thwarts him by putting hat and coat there. Then, carefully moving case and carrier-bag to her left, she sits in the middle of settee.

(Without an option sitting in easy-chair DR) As I should have been. You made a lovely bride.

CLAIRE: *(Pleased)* You're just saying that! Our Daphne was always the really attractive one. You picked the right sister.

TOM: *(Gloomily)* Looks like it, doesn't it? Living on my own in that poky little flat. No room to swing the cat.

CLAIRE: I didn't know you had... I wish you'd have let me go there.

TOM: No, I couldn't... it's such a mess.

CLAIRE: You have your Sally there.

TOM: There is a difference.

CLAIRE: *(Rising uneasily and moving DLC)* It just doesn't seem right... us being here like this together... the two of us.

TOM: There was nowhere else, was there?

CLAIRE: *(Reluctantly)* I suppose not... with Mother living with me. At least it made someone to look after the children.

TOM: Where did you say you were going?

CLAIRE: I'm glad she didn't ask. And I couldn't very well tell the kids I was spending the weekend with their Uncle Tom.

TOM: *(Laughing)* If not in his cabin. It's a good job when Sally told me about staying with her friend she mentioned that Daphne wouldn't be here. *(Rising)* Things couldn't have worked about better. Right, times up!

CLAIRE: *(Tentatively)* Tom!

TOM: What?

CLAIRE: Couldn't we stay down here? I mean, that bedroom... well it was yours and Daphne's. It just doesn't seem right!

TOM: No problem - we'll use Sally's room.

CLAIRE: Won't she mind?

TOM: *(Amused)* She would if she knew... me and her Aunty Claire.

CLAIRE: I shall never be able to look her in the face again - either of them. Especially our Daphne!

TOM: Of course you will. They'll never know - unless you tell them. *(Moving to door R)*

CLAIRE: Tom!

TOM: *(Checking)* Now what is it?

CLAIRE: *(Slowly)* I've been thinking....

TOM: That is dangerous.

CLAIRE: *(Hesitantly)* This will probably sound a bit indelicate, coming at a time like this, but...

TOM: But what?

CLAIRE: I'm absolutely famished.

TOM: Famished?!

CLAIRE: You see, the thing is - I've had no tea. I've had nothing since a sandwich at lunch-time. Friday's late night closing. I only had time to get washed and changed before meeting you at the bus station.

TOM: Well, I've no idea what might be in the fridge - that Daphne wouldn't miss.

CLAIRE: No, that's alright. *(Picking up carrier-bag)* I brought some things from the supermarket before we closed. I thought a little snack - a salad say, and some cold meat. What do you think?

TOM: *(Unenthusiastically)* Sounds great!

CLAIRE: No onions of course - unless we both have some. *(Examining contents of carrier-bag)* There's a bottle of wine - it's only Australian. And passion-fruit for afters.

TOM: *(Aside)* Afters! *(To her)* I can't wait.

CLAIRE: Of course, if you'd rather not... I should understand, but...

TOM: *(Mock-jovially)* No, no, wouldn't want you passing out on me when...

CLAIRE: *(Giggling)* It would be embarrassing.

TOM: So, back to the kitchen. *(As she starts to pick up hat and coat from settee)* Leave them there, nobody's going to run off with them.

CLAIRE: *(Continuing to pick them up)* I can't abide to see a room looking untidy.

TOM: You're a proper fusspot.

CLAIRE: That's what Godfrey used to say - only he said bloody fusspot. *(Encumbered with hat, coat and carrier-bag, she starts to lift her suitcase)*

TOM: Leave it.

CLAIRE: I can manage. *(As she lifts the case its handle slips out of her grasp and it hits the floor with a loud thump)*

TOM: I said "Leave it". *(Moving to pick it up)* Any eggs?

CLAIRE: *(Seriously)* They're in here. *(Indicating carrier-bag; moving to open* *door L)* Bring your rucksack, Tom.

TOM: It's alright... *(As she looks fixedly at him)* I'll bring the rucksack! *(As CLAIRE EXITS L he collects rucksack from DR, slings it onto a shoulder and moves below settee to pick up suitcase)* Perhaps I should have gone hiking! *(Exits L and closes door behind him)*

After a few seconds the door R opens and SALLY ENTERS, peering cautiously in with the door only partly open. Seeing the room to be empty she opens door fully and moves in, followed by NEAL who is carrying empty glass. His hair is ruffled and tie slightly askew.

SALLY: *(Moving UC)* I was sure I heard a noise down here, didn't you?

NEAL: *(Closing door and moving URC)* I wasn't listening.

SALLY: *(Moving L of settee)* We were only kissing.

NEAL: What sort of noise?

SALLY: A sort of loud thump, like something falling.

NEAL: *(Moving DRC)* There's no body here.

SALLY: I can see that.

NEAL: I meant a corpse.

SALLY: You've been reading too much Agatha Christie.

NEAL: I don't care much for thrillers.

SALLY: I suppose your idea of a good read is curling up in bed with Jackie Collins or Jilly Cooper.

NEAL: Who?

SALLY: Never mind. And what's the glass for? Not more water!

NEAL: *(Moving below settee)* I thought I'd take it back into the kitchen.

SALLY: No, you don't! *(Moving quickly to L of him)* Give it to me. *(Taking it from him)* You wouldn't be able to resist putting it under the tap again. *(Moving to put glass onto sideboard L)* I must have been mistaken about the noise. Perhaps you'd set my heart pounding. *(Moving above settee to door R)* Let's see if you can do it again! *(Starting to open door and then closing it quickly; apprehensively)* There's someone coming down the stairs!

As she backs away with eyes fixed firmly on the door NEAL panics, considers escaping through the door L but then moves quickly to hide behind the L half of the floor-length curtains. The door R opens slowly and DAPHNE looks cautiously into the room, still in her negligee.

DAPHNE: }*(In surprised unison)* Sally! What are you doing here?

SALLY: } Mother! What are you doing here?

SALLY: *(Awkwardly)* I thought I heard something.

DAPHNE: So did I. *(Closing door)* But what I did mean was what are you doing back here on your own?

SALLY: On my... *(glancing behind her; aside)* Now where's he gone?

DAPHNE: What are you looking for?

SALLY: *(Feigning)* I was wondering what could have made that noise.

DAPHNE: *(Firmly)* Never mind the noise - probably Tommy next door. Why aren't you at your father's?

SALLY: At father's? *(Moving away above settee to ULC as she plays for time to think. Seeing the empty glass on the sideboard L she moves to pick it up and mimes draining the non-existent contents)* Gosh, I was thirsty! *(Putting glass back on sideboard)*

DAPHNE: *(Persisting as moves DRC)* I asked why aren't you with your father?

SALLY: *(Moving DLC with sudden inspiration)* He's got the flu.

DAPHNE: The flu! Why didn't he ring and let me know?

SALLY: *(Continuing to improvise)* It came on very suddenly - just before I got there. One minute he was apparently quite alright and the next he felt he was knocking at death's door.

DAPHNE: *(Tartly)* Death should have opened it!

SALLY: He said I'd better not stay... not with all those nasty little germs floating about... *(using her hands to demonstrate as she wonders what has happened to Neal)* all over the place.

DAPHNE: *(Suspiciously)* Are you alright? You're behaving very strangely.

SALLY: Am I? It must have been the shock - of seeing you here.

DAPHNE: But I suppose he thought I shouldn't be?

SALLY: I believe I might have mentioned it - in passing. *(As DAPHNE starts to* *move above settee towards L)* What are you going to do?

DAPHNE: *(Hotly)* Phone to let him know precisely what I think of him... as if he doesn't already know!

SALLY: *(Desperately)* I shouldn't do that.

DAPHNE: Why not? He's a fine father, letting you come to spend the weekend on your own in an empty house.

SALLY: But I'm not, am I? *(Glancing thoughtfully to door L)* You're here. And he said he was going to take two aspirins and go to bed.

DAPHNE: Why not the whole bottle!

SALLY: It wouldn't be fair to wake him up, would it?

DAPHNE: *(Grudgingly)* I suppose not... *(moving L of settee to below and then sitting)* though I am tempted.

SALLY: Anyway, what are you doing back here?

DAPHNE: *(Aware of Timothy's presence and glancing apprehensively R)* It's a long story... and I'm not sure where to start.

NEAL pops his head out from behind the curtain and attracts Sally's attention. Moving ULC, behind Daphne's back, SALLY mimes that she is going to open door R and that he should tip-toe out, go upstairs, get his hat, coat, scarf, rattle and travel-bag, tip-toe back downstairs and out of the front door.

(As SALLY moves above settee and opens door R; with alarm) You're not going upstairs?

SALLY: I thought it had got stuffy in here. *(Fanning herself)*

DAPHNE: Now it's cold. I'm only wearing this negligee. Close it, please, Sally.

SALLY: *(Reluctantly closing door and moving above settee to wave Neal back behind the curtain)* Were you going to bed? *(DAPHNE reacts)* Is that why you came home... because you weren't feeling well?

DAPHNE: *(With sudden inspiration)* Perhaps it's the flu! I think you'd better go and stay with your Aunty Claire for the weekend.

SALLY: *(Thinking desperately as she moves DLC)* She may be out.

NEAL pops his head out again and, with urgency, mimes that he is about to hiccup and points to the glass on the sideboard L.

DAPHNE: *(As SALLY moves to sideboard L to pick up the glass)* I hardly think so. She doesn't get out much. What with working at the supermarket, looking after the children - and with your Gran living with her. *(SALLY upturning the glass to demonstrate it being empty turns to show NEAL who, having clamped a hand to his mouth to suppress a hiccup, has disappeared again behind the curtain)* Poor Claire! She could do with a man in her life - but heaven knows how she's going to get one. No wonder Godfrey ran off with that traffic-warden. Probably thought it would end up cheaper than keep getting fined. *(Turning to see SALLY still holding the upturned glass)* What on earth are you doing?

SALLY: *(For Neal's benefit)* It's empty.

DAPHNE: Of course it's empty - you emptied it.

SALLY: I'll get some more. I'm still thirsty. *(Moving towards door L)*

DAPHNE: What have you been eating - crisps?

NEAL hiccups from behind the curtain. DAPHNE half-turns, sensing that the noise came from behind her.

SALLY: *(Pretending it came from her)* Pardon!

DAPHNE: *(Accusingly)* You have been eating crisps.

SALLY: *(Now reluctant to leave in case Neal hiccups again and 'inventing' conversation)* You haven't fallen out with him, have you?

DAPHNE: Who?

SALLY: The W... Mr Wainwright.

DAPHNE: *(Becoming worried)* Certainly not!

SALLY: *(Moving UC as NEAL again pops out his head and indicates growing desperation)* I should have thought you were too old for lovers' tiffs. *(Gesticulating to Neal)*

DAPHNE: *(Rising quickly and moving DLC)* Too old! What gave you the idea we were lovers? Timothy - Mr Wainwright and I are just good friends.

SALLY: When am I going to meet him?

DAPHNE: *(Vaguely as she turns upstage and NEAL quickly disappears behind the curtain)* Oh... soon. *(Flatly as she sees door R start to open)* Very soon!

TIMOTHY ENTERS R, now only wearing shirt and tie, Y-fronts and socks held up by suspenders. Leaving door open and looking quite ridiculous he limps painfully in to DRC.

TIMOTHY: *(Looking at Daphne)* Don't start anything without me, you said. I've been on the starting-blocks that long I've got cramp in my... *(as she frantically tries to make him aware of Sally)* why are you waving like that? *(Eventually turning to see Sally)* Oh! *(He 'freezes')*

DAPHNE: *(Wishing earth would open and swallow her)* This is my daughter, Sally. *(To Sally)* Meet Mr Wainwright.

The curtain L moves slightly but remains unnoticed in the tense situation.

TIMOTHY: *(Starting to move towards Sally with an outstretched hand but then, suddenly realising his state of undress, he drops it quickly and covers his groin with both hands)* Excuse me! *(Moving awkwardly crab-wise he moves to door and Exits R, closing door behind him)*

SALLY: *(Highly amused as she moves DRC)* Just good friends!

DAPHNE: *(Defensively)* More or less... in a manner of speaking.

SALLY: What would Daddy say if he knew?

DAPHNE: *(Sharply)* It's none of his business! *(As a gentle plea)* Besides he won't know, will he?... unless you tell him.

She is looking directly at Sally as NEAL hiccups loudly from behind the curtain.

That wasn't you!

SALLY: *(Trying to feign)* What wasn't?

DAPHNE: You know very well. *(Starting to move ULC)* There's someone behind that curtain.

SALLY: *(With quiet resignation)* You'd better come out, Neal. *(He does so slowly and utterly embarrassed)* Neal, this is my mother. Mummy, this is Neal. We're...

DAPHNE: *(Looking him up and down disapprovingly)* Just good friends, I suppose.

NEAL: *(In obvious discomfort)* Sorry, I shall have to go to the... *(hiccups)* toilet. *(Moving quickly to open door R and Exit, leaving door open)*

DAPHNE: *(Severely)* Well, young lady, what have you got to say?

SALLY: *(Moving to close door)* I did keep telling him not to drink all that water. *(Displaying empty glass)*

DAPHNE: *(Moving below settee)* I wasn't referring to his drinking habits - or weak bladder. What have you two been doing?

SALLY: *(To DRC)* Nothing, Mummy. *(Weakly)* Well, hardly anything. Only kissing. And he's not very good. He needs more practice.

DAPHNE: Which no doubt he was going to get! I really am surprised at you, Sally - and disappointed.

SALLY: *(Sadly)* So am I! It wasn't much fun.

DAPHNE: Did you pick him up somewhere on the way back from your father's flat?

SALLY: *(Hotly as she moves above settee to ULC)* I didn't pick him up! *(Feigning)* I - er, I phoned him when I got back here... so I wouldn't be here on my own. *(Putting glass on sideboard)*

DAPHNE: This is all your father's fault... getting the flu! You should have phoned me at Mr Wainwright's - I gave you the number.

SALLY: What good would that have done? You're both here. *(Moving DLC)* That's alright, isn't it? You and him!

DAPHNE: That's completely different. Timothy and I are both fully-grown adults - *(aside)* at least I am! You're only sixteen, Sally.

SALLY: Nearly seventeen.

DAPHNE: *(Sympathetically)* I know, darling. You know, you really shouldn't take your example from what I do. *(Aside)* Or in the present instance haven't done - don't look like doing! *(Thoughtfully; to her)* Although I can see it might be my fault.

SALLY: *(Intensely as she moves to L of her)* No, it isn't! It's just that... *(hesitantly)* well, all the other girls in the class said that they'd... you know... done it. *(With feeling)* Though I don't believe Mavis Oldthorpe for one minute. *(With girlish spite)* I mean, whoever would...

DAPHNE: *(Taking her in her arms)* Darling, you shouldn't worry your pretty little head about what other girls do, or don't do - even if it is true. What matters - the only thing that does matter - is that you do only what you know is right. And there's plenty of time. There's no need to rush. You have all the time in the world. *(More lightly)* And when it is time I suggest it might be better with someone other than Neal. He doesn't strike me as ever being one of the world's great lovers. *(Aside)* And I should know! So what do you say? *(Kissing her)*

SALLY: *(Hugging her warmly and kissing her back)* Thanks, you're the bestest mum in the whole wide world!

The door R opens and NEAL ENTERS, wearing his anorak and scarf and carrying hat, rattle and travel-bag.

NEAL: *(In open doorway)* I'll be getting along home now, Sally.

SALLY: *(Breaking out of embrace and crossing below Daphne to R of settee)* You can't.

NEAL: *(Embarrassed)* I can't stay here now, can I? *(Nodding pointedly towards Daphne)* Besides, he's here, isn't he? *(Now nodding pointedly to Offstage R)*

SALLY: If you're not careful your head will drop off! *(Kindly)* You can't go home, Neal, you're supposed to be on your way to London.

NEAL: *(Miserably)* Oh, aye, I forgot. I could say I missed the bus.

SALLY: You were going by train. *(He dumbly agrees)*

DAPHNE: He'd better stay here the night. He can sleep on the settee.

SALLY: *(Jollying him)* There, you see! Thanks, Mum. So close the door and sit yourself down.

NEAL closes the door and SALLY, taking his arm in friendly fashion, brings him downstage to easy-chair DR. He puts down his travel-bag and is standing with hat and rattle in hand as door L opens and TOM ENTERS breezily and then his mouth opens at the scene he witnesses.

(Surprised) Daddy! *(This causes DAPHNE to swing round L)*

TOM: *(Equally surprised)* Sally!

DAPHNE: *(Also surprised)* Tom!

TOM: *(Shocked)* Daphne!

SALLY: }

TOM: } *(In unison)* What are you doing here?

DAPHNE: }

TOM: Ladies first!

DAPHNE: Don't try to be polite... it doesn't suit you! I thought you'd got the flu.

TOM: *(Baffled)* Got the flu?

DAPHNE: Sally said you'd gone to bed with a couple of aspirins.

TOM: But I haven't... *(Moving in to DLC and looking towards Sally)* I thought you were...

SALLY: *(Moving quickly below Daphne to R of him)* Worried about you? I was - terribly worried about you. *(Throwing her arms around his neck)* Was it a false alarm? *(With emphasis)* It was a false alarm, wasn't it, Daddy?

TOM: *(Joining in the conspiracy)* That's right, a false alarm. I took a couple of aspirins and felt a lot better. So I took two more and felt better still. *(Whispering to her)* I thought you were at your friend's?

SALLY: *(Whispering back)* I'll explain later. *(Removing her arms; aloud)* So you came to see how I was? *(Crossing below him to DL)*

TOM: *(Moving to L of Daphne)* That's right, I came to see how she was on her own. *(Becoming aware of Neal)* Who's he?

DAPHNE: That's Neal. He's a friend of Sally's.

TOM: What time's the kick-off? Is he coming or going?

DAPHNE: He was going.

SALLY: But now he's staying.

TOM: *(Crossing below Daphne to L of Neal)* Doesn't say much, does he? *(To Neal)* I should sit down, son. You're making the place untidy. *(He does so)* You can take your scarf off if you like. *(He does so and lays it on his lap together with hat and rattle. Tom turns to Daphne)* If I'd known you were here I shouldn't have come... to see about Sally, I mean. *(Winking across at her and she winks back)* I thought you were away.

DAPHNE: *(Now uneasy)* I was... but I came back. I wasn't feeling very well. *(Indicating negligee)* I was just going to have a bath, *(with emphasis)* wasn't I,. Sally? *(Quickly before she can reply)* So now you know she's alright, you can be getting back, can't you?

TOM: *(Only too eager)* That's right. *(Crossing below Daphne to R of Sally)* See you next Friday, sugar.

The door R opens and TIMOTHY ENTERS, now fully dressed.

TIMOTHY: *(As he enters)* That's better, now I'm dressed again! *(Checking)* Oh, I see you've got company, Daphne. *(Stands looking uncomfortable)*

DAPHNE: *(Gesturing R)* That is Neal - he's a friend of Sally's.

TIMOTHY: *(Moving DRC, then suddenly stopping as he recognises Neal; to himself)* Oh, dear, oh dear! It's Tankersley, isn't it?

NEAL: *(Jumping up quickly and letting contents of his lap fall to floor)* Yes, sir.

DAPHNE: *(To both of them)* Do you two know each other?

NEAL: *(Blurting out)* It's the W... it's Mr Wainwright. He used to teach me mathematics.

TIMOTHY: I used to try! Sit down, boy - I mean, Neal. We're not in school now, are we?

NEAL: No, sir. *(Sitting and recovering items from floor)*

TIMOTHY: *(Perching himself on L arm of easy-chair and adopting a confidential attitude)* Now, Neal, as man to man you haven't seen me here, have you?

NEAL: Yes, sir.

TIMOTHY: No, you haven't! Do you understand? *(He appears to be the opposite)* It's quite simple. I am not here... I have never been here! I cannot have word of this being bandied about the neighbourhood. What would all the parents think? Now I may have been somewhat unfair to you in the past... a little harsh perhaps... but it was for your own good, Tankersley - your algebra particularly was deplorable.

NEAL: *(Forthrightly)* You used to say I couldn't tell an x from a y!

TIMOTHY: *(Attempting jocularity)* Did I say that? Just my little joke. *(Patting his arm in a friendly manner and then standing)* I'm glad we understand each other. *(To Daphne)* Sorry about that - always nice to meet a former star pupil.

DAPHNE: And Tim, this is Tom *(gesturing L)* ... Tom, this is Tim. *(As Timothy appears to be going to cross to shake hands)* Tom is my husband. *(TIMOTHY* *checks quickly)* Tom came to see whether Sally was alright on her own - but she wasn't... on her own, I mean. So he's leaving, *(pointedly)* aren't you, Tom?

TOM: *(Deliberately being provocative)* Am I?

DAPHNE: *(Sharply)* Well, aren't you?

TIMOTHY: *(Uneasily)* Perhaps I should leave?

DAPHNE: *(Annoyed)* Where would you go?

TIMOTHY: To the flat, of course.

DAPHNE: Stanley's got that woman there.

TIMOTHY: I was forgetting her.

DAPHNE: Perhaps she wouldn't mind a threesome? After all, Stanley is handicapped. An extra hand might be useful.

TIMOTHY: *(Pompously)* Daphne! I find that remark most objectionable.

DAPHNE: Then you'd better stay here. I shouldn't want you walking the streets, being picked up by the police and getting your name in the papers.

TIMOTHY: *(Shuddering)* Certainly not!

DAPHNE: You can sleep in the easy-chair. *(Indicating DR where Neal is sitting)*

TIMOTHY: What's wrong with the settee? *(Indicating empty settee)*

DAPHNE: That's already reserved for Neal. *(TIMOTHY turns to look disdainfully at him)*

TOM: *(Flippantly)* Perhaps they could swap over at half-time? Well, now that the accommodation problem is sorted out, I'll be leaving. *(Cheerfully)* Have a nice weekend everybody. *(Turning to leave L)*

CLAIRE: *(Offstage L)* I'm ready when you are, Tom!

TOM 'freezes' and all react. The door L opens and CLAIRE ENTERS, having altered her hair to something more attractive. She is gingerly carrying an unopened bottle of wine.

(As she enters) Haven't you found the corkscrew yet? *(Giving a scream as she sees all the others, causing the bottle to leave her hands in an upwards direction)*

TOM: *(Leaping forward to catch the bottle and then juggle with it as if unable* *to hold it)* It's like ice!

CLAIRE: I thought I'd put it in the freezer to chill it quickly.

TOM: *(Juggling with it and moving to deposit it on sideboard L)* Chill it? It'll be frozen solid. We shan't need the corkscrew... just the hammer and chisel!

DAPHNE: *(As CLAIRE stands shame-faced, not knowing what to do with herself)* Claire! What exactly are you doing here with Tom? *(Hastily)* Omit the exactly!

SALLY: *(Upset)* Daddy! How could you - with Aunty Claire?

CLAIRE: *(Woefully)* Oh, Tom, I knew we shouldn't have come here!

DAPHNE: *(Turning on Sally)* And where did your father think you were? Not here quite obviously!

TOM: *(Unperturbed at the situation; to Sally)* Yes, young lady, why aren't you with Mavis Oldthorpe like you told me?

As she hesitates with all eyes on her, MRS TOMKINS ENTERS UC (from Offstage L) outside the windows. Her mouth drops open as she looks in and then, recovering, she raps urgently on the window frame.

Ignore her! She'll go away.

MRS TOMKINS raps again, gesticulating frantically and mouthing unheard.

DAPHNE: *(Resignedly)* I'd better see what she wants. *(Moving R of settee to UC)*

TOM: *(Tersely)* I know what she wants!

DAPHNE: *(Opens the windows to allow her to step inside to L)* What is it, Mrs Tomkins?

MRS TOMKINS: *(Spookily)* I 'eard voices!

TOM: She's been drinking again!

MRS TOMKINS: I knew as 'ow you was supposed to be away for the weekend.

TOM: Surprise, surprise!

MRS TOMKINS: So I thought as 'ow you was being burglaried.

DAPHNE: *(Trying to be patient)* That was very thoughtful of you. But as you can see we're not.

MRS TOMKINS: *(Defensively)* I was only doin' my duty as 'ow any caring neighbour should.

DAPHNE: And I want you to know how much I appreciate that. *(Trying to gently shepherd her back out of the windows)* We all do, don't we? *(Turning back to the others from whom there is no response)* Goodnight, Mrs Tomkins, and sleep tight.

TOM: Mind the bugs don't bite! *(DAPHNE turns to glare at him)*

MRS TOMKINS: *(Moving back inside)* There is one other thing. I suppose as 'ow you ought to know... I rang for the police.

ALL: *(Amidst general reaction)* The police!

NEAL jumps to his feet, again spilling the items from his lap.

DAPHNE: *(With a total change of attitude)* Why can't you mind your own business, you nosey old bag!

MRS TOMKINS: *(Affronted)* Well, I likes that, I must say! All the thanks I get!

SOUND OF POLICE-CAR SIREN (Offstage)

Sounds like they're here. I'll be off! *(Exits UC to offstage L)*

As NEAL picks up the items off the floor trying to make a quick escape, the rattle gives a rattle.

TOM: Sounds as if somebody's scored.

CLAIRE: Oh, Tom! I did say we shouldn't do it.

TOM: *(With feeling)* We haven't done it! I might as well have gone hiking.

SIREN BECOMES LOUDER

CLAIRE: *(Wailing)* Now we shall all be in Sunday's "News of the World"!

SIREN BECOMES LOUDER STILL.

CURTAIN

Other NPN Plays by Jack Booth
Full Length Plays

343 A Question of Identity 3M 3F

Lance returns home after years abroad to claim his share of the inheritance left solely to his identical twin brother Gyles. A struggle ensues during which Gyles is killed and Lance assumes his identity. The headless corpse at first appears to offer no threat. However when a second body is discovered his newly-acquired past poses a problem for Lance from which there is no escape.

254 Sleeping Arrangements 4M 3F

Hollywood star Kathleen Fenton is upset when, visiting England with prospective husband number 3, she discovers as her mother's guest ex-husband number 1. Her annoyance grows as the men hit it off and plan filming together. When Kathleen's glamour photographer father arrives with a model in tow and ex-husband number 2 appears, the general tension increases with sleeping arrangements becoming of paramount concern.

332 Tangled Web 3M 3F

Ex-mercenary soldier Ian Millward has heavy gambling debts. Now a photojournalist, he ostensibly arranges to interview wealthy Sir Robert Darwent but actually intends to blackmail him over revealing photographs taken of his wife Anne years ago when Ian's lover. But Sir Robert also has a past indiscretion to hide and Ian increasingly finds himself enmeshed, leading to a highly dramatic and unforeseen dénouement.

One Act Plays

300 By Whose Hand 5F

On an evening in the late 1940's the Fairclough women leave the menfolk to their after-dinner drinks. The drawing-room tranquility is broken by the arrival of a German-speaking woman seeking revenge for her sister's murder during the war. One of three men in the house was the killer. Amidst revelations and rising tensions the question is... by whose hand?

257 Dead On Time 1M 3F

A wealthy but ruthless industrialist is being the victim of threatening phone calls. He is told that by two o'clock next morning he will be a dead man. The police are called in and members of his household are questioned. The deadline approaches but nothing untoward occurs. Is it the work of a crank... or may he still be "dead on time"!?

314 Echo of Applause 3M 2F

On a provincial stage the show is over - closure and demolition will follow. Tony has vainly struggled to save both theatre and his blighted career. In despair he seeks the solace of alcohol and rejects one woman's advances. Tony himself may be saved by a girl's innocent love but the theatre will be left with its ghosts and an echo of applause.

316 Friendly Affair 4F

Newly-pregnant and highly-strung Glenda has a problem - suspicious lipstick on her husband's collar. Panic-stricken, she summons for help - her more experienced older sister, her man-loving best friend and the dominant wife of Martin's best friend in whom he may have confided his infidelity. Misunderstandings follow and unfriendly accusations are made before the surprise dénouement leaves Glenda covered with embarrassment.

312 Little White Lies 3M 3F

Laura 'invents' a visit to a friend in Brighton to explain the unexpected arrival at her parents' house. This arouses sister Muriel's suspicions regarding the Brighton conference husband Clive was to attend. In retaliation Laura and Clive stage a seduction scene which backfires with the arrival of husband Alan. Another little white lie is revealed when it transpires that Muriel and Alan had spent a night.... together? The plot thickens!

306 The Loved One 1M 2F

Lewis met Jane in Paris and romance briefly blossomed. Visiting her to renew the relationship he learns of Edward, her dead fiancé. A servant says he was engaged to the sister of whom Jane was insanely jealous and may have been responsible for the accident that killed them both. Lewis hastily retreats, leaving Jane fantasising of a Paris honeymoon with her loved one - Edward.

328 Season of Goodwill 3M 4F

Northerner Alfred, Works Foreman, has a new manager and neighbour, Humphrey, from the South. Amicable relations exist until Alfred's anticipated quiet Christmas without his mother-in-law. Humphrey's cockerel goes crowing berserk and in distraction Alfred does likewise. The rift escalates when Alfred vetoes the engagement of their respective offspring and finds himself isolated. Unexpected events conspire to heal the wounds but Alfred still has a problem.

239 Seeing Double 1M 3F

Attempting to end an affair, Quentin sends Lysette unknowingly to twin brother Justin for him to see her as Quentin with the latter liaising unseen through an internal intercom system. With Justin's wife mistaking Lysette as a new medical patient and Quentin's suspicious wife turning up the plan goes wrong causing "both brothers" to make ever-increasing frantic appearances in one guise or the other.

253 Two Sides of a Square 1M 3F

Maggie and Ernest share a successful relationship, each living alone on opposite sides of a town square. Ernest's carefree existence is shattered by Maggie's announcement that they should live together and start a family. Complications ensue with the intrusions of Nadine, Ernest's nubile new neighbour, and - across the square - the voyeur Miss Hebblewhite convinced that Ernest is a would-be rapist.